Heartache and Constellations

Blossom Alley

Presentation by *BookLeaf Publishing*

Web: www.bookleafpub.com

E-mail: info@bookleafpub.com

ISBN: 9789357445474

First edition 2021

DEDICATION

I dedicate this to the person who is sat next to me as I am writing this dedication - you encourage me to push my boundaries and to be brave.

You know who you are.

Doubt

I'm not going to drown my fears
To try to hide from the grip of my chest
The spiralling whirlpool of my thoughts,

I've tried it before,
And all bubbles float to the surface,
Drowning leaves you gasping for air.

I'm afraid,
Afraid that I will end up with nothing,
That my tears, anger and the long, long nights
Will leave me alone
And wondering what the fucking point was.

I hate the fact that I'm so unsure,
Unsure if I'm letting my fear fabricate far-off
stories,
Unsure if I'm letting my fear bend my trust in
you
In order to protect from being too naive
Too young
Too blind,

Maybe it's my fear of being wrong,
Of being wrong in front of my peers,

Of being wrong in my faith,

A self-fulfilling Prophet

Because it feels better to be in control

With you I'm not in control of my emotions
Because you mean so much
The chest takes over.
The whirlpool takes over.

We make plans over the phone and they feel like
empty promises,
I look at photos of you and I don't know what I
feel
Maybe I'm becoming numb because these last
months have been too painful for this
To be sustainable.
Or maybe I'm getting over you.
Who knows.

I'd like to think it's all in my head
Because then when you get back everything will
be good
And I can look back to now and know that
It was all for something

Only one way to find out

A Sign

I'm crying
Tears are cascading down my cheeks,
Curled up in your arms
Stalagmites in my nose
Pooling on your shirt.

I'm tired from last night,
You were drunk,
I was not,
You were off and
I was working.
The "good luck" drinks from our coworkers had
left you
With cotton mouth,
And a bitter taste in mine.

As your wide blue eyes search mine,
Trying to figure out how to soothe my pain,
I wonder,
Why you aren't finding this as hard as I am,

You pull some silly faces,
Trying to tug a smile from my lips,
But it doesn't work.
Not this time.

I sob some more,
And you pull me closer,
Lying down,
I notice a single teardrop
Roll down your nose.

Only then do I feel better.

Blurs

I hate this feeling
I can't hug you
I can only sit in this silence
And wait for late night calls
That steal my sleep

How long do I wait until
The comfort of your silence grows
Into yet another bullet that my chest doesn't
want.

I wonder if
Again
I'm sacrificing too much of my time
For men
Who wouldn't do the same.
The knots in my back
Keep my arms numb from the pain.

Tears fall down my face
In place of words.
Smudging the ink
And the story blurs

A Tipsy and very Cringey Poem

It's always you,

You make me feel like waves crashing on to the
beach,
Unpredictable,
A visionary,
The same but new.

I think that maybe,
Just maybe,
I fall.
I fall from what I feel,
Whirlpool.

Deep into my thoughts,
My fears,
And it manifests,

Manifests into my castle walls,
Trapping myself,
Trying to protect from some sort of ancient
battle,

The war of keeping myself safe and
Letting myself love you.

Because loving you isn't safe,
It isn't the known.
And that's so, so scary.

But you are worth it.

You are my light.

You are the playful grin on my lips when I've
Had a little bit too much
Liquor.
You are my unpredictable humour,
Bringing forth bellows from the depths of my
abdomen,
Reminding me that I can be happy,
Be full,
Like the pulsating arteries that
Course through my ever-fighting body.

You are the quiet breeze,
On a warm summers day,

I love you.

I love you the freakin' mostest.

Halves

It's been four days.

I'm sitting in the bath looking at my silly tan
lines.

They remind me of the holiday with your family
two months ago,
And the holiday we were supposed to go on in
two days

Just the two of us.

But now it is one month until my birthday,
And what would've been our one year
anniversary,
Which is one day before.

You've left me with only half of myself

Bedtime

I know that with a little bit of time,
And a little bit of luck,
That I'm gonna find someone else.
That I'll have a new warmth in my life,
And I'll be thankful that you didn't want me
Because it led me to them.

The thing is, I don't fucking want to.

Because at the end of the day,
Just before I go to bed,
It's you I miss.

It really sucks that you don't feel the same.

Nipple Piercings

I got nipple piercings on Monday.

It was 3 o'clock
And I strolled down to the
Tattoo shop that can be found

To get two needles stuck in my breast
Cos they felt better than the pins and needles in
my chest

Because with those I can't breathe.
Aaaaaand the cigarettes don't help.

The cigarettes that I use (abuse)
To fight those god damn winter blues
And to forget that I ever needed you
And to forget the fact that I still kinda do.

It's been four months.

Four months since you broke my heart,
The one that was already falling apart
Which left me filling the wrong holes
With coworkers and bumble,
When I'm feeling bold

And food and blankets when I'm feeling cold
And alone.

I guess…

I guess I'm just trying to get by
On the days where all I do is cry
And wait for all this time to fly
To the day that it gets better.

Because it will,
I'm betting on it.

Adam? I Think?

It's my first snog in a while

You were from worthing,
And I think your name was Adam,
And my head and body,
are saying "you could've had him"

But your mates said you were taken
Was it a joke?
You are who you surrounded by
So what kind of bloke
Are you?

Because cheating isn't funny.

I think of my ex
I think that all he loved
Was my body and the sex
That was readily available when he was with
me.
And in the co-worker he chose over me.

The bartender I was flirting with -
Who I could have chosen over you -
I KNOW his name

It was Connor.

But I was drunk,
And he was sober,
And I don't know if he was single,
Or getting over

Some unbeknownst to me
Ex, or not ex, lover.
My broken heart and
My sore chest wants to take cover.

So I've left the club,
And now I walk home,
Still drunk from the shots
And still fucking alone.

Pen Pals

Pen Pals

You're the first person I've talked to in 6 months
Who hasn't made me feel nervous once
That everything I say is coming from the mouth
Of a complete and utter dunce.

Even if by talking
I mean messaging
As I've yet to hear your voice.

I'm comfortable,
Even excited to see your username,
The username I've yet to change
Because it has only been like 3 or 4 days
And I don't want Jinx it

Because I'm waiting for the catch,
And if I change it to your first name
I'll latch onto hope that this is
Something more than just another Bumble
match.

But yet I'm feeling safer
Less weary of what lies in store

Safer than of the men before you.
And after him.

Is this gonna hurt?

Maybe.

Am I gonna keep doing it anyway?

Probably.

Either way,
No matter what tomorrow brings my way
I'm just gonna enjoy these 3 or 4 days
While I ca

Patterns

I thought that this time might be different.
But no.
In the back of my mind
I knew how this would go.

Stuck again,
Moping about some boy
Who for like 5 minutes
Gave me temporary joy

The tight chest
When his name lit up my phone
And yet here I am
And I'm still fucking alone.

Why aren't I good enough?
Why do I give them a time of day?
Because although they're different guys
It all hurts the same way.

I dunno.

It just feels like every time
I find someone new
They get bored of me and run…

Maybe I should just become a nun.

Escape

It had been a long night.

We had both been going through rough patches,
Yours sounded worse than mine.

I had uni later that day
But it was over an hour away
From your house.

And I reckon that it'll be okay
If I skipped it just once.

Uni comes around all the time,
Moments like this don't

We listen to hopeful music
And watch the cigarette smoke
Dancing in the morning rays
That peek through your blinds

for one hour we let ourselves escape.

... well this was unexpected ...

Well…

This was unexpected.
Could not predict what's next and
It really is good sex and
You're doing things my ex never did.

It's crazy.
And scary.
And… a little bit exciting?

Okay that's a lie,
It's very exciting.

And I'm just here,
Sitting on my bed,
Looking at the flowers,
Thinking of the words that you've said,

And the way that my immediate future has changed,
Seemingly out of nowhere.

Life has its ways.

And I know it has only been two weeks.
And I really don't want to freak
You out
By telling you how invested I am already.

I hope this works

3 more weeks have passed

Still invested.

Hazel Eyed Love

A poem for the one with eyes of hazel,
I'll try to be succinct if I'm able
To sum up everything in a line or two,
The many things that make up
What I love about you.

I love your face,
And the way you make time
For us to wine, dine
And sixty-nine,

I love the way you keep me smiling
A noticeable glow
Radiates out of me
From head to toe

You keep me safe
And warm and sound
I get much heartache when
You're not around

So I thank whoever
Looks down from above
For giving me a wonderful
Hazel eyed love!

Constellation

I trace the constellation on your chest
The Big Dipper pointing to the North Star
The North Star guiding me home.

I think about us
About our pasts
Like the night sky
Littered with complicated events
Each running on their own timelines,
With cataclysmic starts and
Fiery ends
Leaving vast holes within ourselves.

I think about how many of these
Long, long nights it took
To get to the simplicity of just being with you.

You - the one who shines so bright

I have run out of
poems

She sits on the bed,
And lets out a sigh,
Signed up for a challenge,
And didn't realise that the end date was fast
approaching.

And she needed 4 more poems.
In one more day.

Ooops.

So from here on dear reader,
In this book does reside,
A few more nice poems that have a
Thematic divide from the rest of the book.

Whether they turn out better I'll let you decide!

A morning realisation

As I sift through
the list labelled "to do"

And find the empty check mark under
"find someone to fix the sink"
It begins to sink in.

......I am adult.....

When did that happen?

King Kurt Big Cock

A long time ago
There was a great king,
A wonderful lad
The most handsome thing

A eurasian young maiden,
Dressed up in a frock,
Presented him a record
'King Kurt, Big Cock'

He said - "my cock, as long it may be…
Its not Kurt with a K,
It's Curt with a C'